Idea.
Think.
Create.

Julia A. Royston

BK
ROYSTON
Publishing

BK Royston Publishing

P. O. Box 4321

Jeffersonville, IN 47131

502-802-5385

http://www.bkroystonpublishing.com

bkroystonpublishing@gmail.com

Cover Design: Elite Book Covers

Illustrations Licensed through Shutterstock

ISBN-13: 978-1-959543-02-2

Printed in the United States of America

Dedication

This is dedicated to all Creatives. Let's go!

This is also dedicated to my parents, Dr. Jack and Mrs. Daisy Foree who recognized my creativity as a child and never once tried to discredit it, slow it down or stop it. They educated me to have a job with a pension to fund my creativity.

Love you and Thank you Forever.

Table of Contents

Introduction

I believe that I have been a creative all of my life. I first sang at the age of eight years old. I was a choir director by 12. I was in band as a flute and piccolo player from 4th grade through college. I didn't write my first song until 40. I didn't release my first book until 44.

My parents always encouraged me in everything that I did musically or academically. Now at 59, I am living out my dream and writing like crazy. At this stage in my life, I want to encourage creative young people everywhere to do as much as you can while you're young. Don't wait until you're my age to go for it. Sure, have money to live and pay bills, but always work on your craft. Always find time to do what you're passionate about. If you work hard, one day, you will be able to do what you love full-time, watch it pay off and reward you.

Let's Create!

All About the Author

All books start with the author. No matter whether the character, the dialogue, the action, the ending or the 10 or 20 things that you want to tell your audience in a non-fiction book comes first, it all starts with you, the author, the writer and the creator of the book.

In fiction, the characters will tell the story and you'll be the scribe. In non-fiction, your experience may tell the story and you will just recall the things that you've seen and heard.

No matter what, it starts with you. As a creative, you need to some times take a step back, review and re-discover who you are now compared to who you were before. It will surprise you how much you've changed, evolved and grown. Let's go and find out about you, the author!

ALL ABOUT ME

**Write and illustrate.
Then introduce yourself**

My name

My birthday

My pets

My family

My school

My friends

My city

My favorite food

My favorite subject

My hobbies

Introduce Yourself

Put your name, and create an acrostic poem of positive words with the letters of your name

For Example...

Merry

Athletic

Runner

Young

All About Me!

This is a picture of me!

All About Me!

This is a picture of my family

All About Me!

My Favorite Book is:

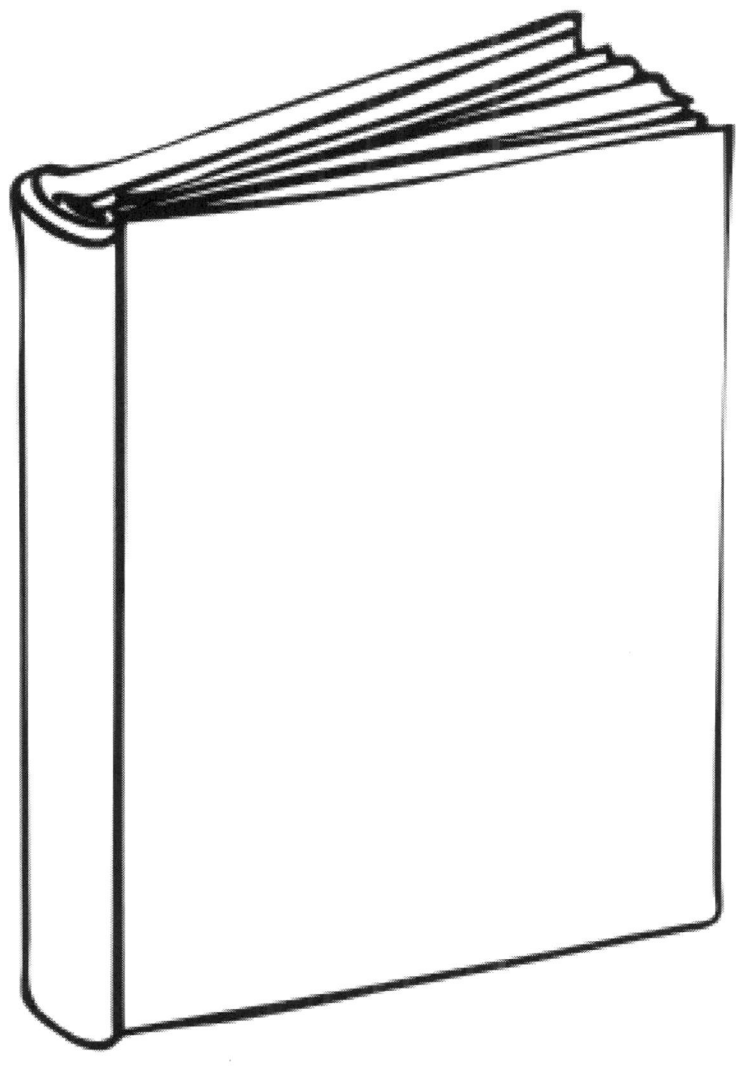

All About Me!

What do you want to be when you grow up?

Write a Story

Write a short story about something on the
"All About Me" Page.

_____

_____

_____

_____

_____

_____

_____

_____

_____

_____

_____

Write a Story

Write a short story about something on the
"All About Me" Page.

_____

_____

_____

_____

_____

_____

_____

_____

_____

_____

Write a Story

Write a short story about something on the
"All About Me" Page.

_____

_____

_____

_____

_____

_____

_____

_____

_____

_____

Write a Story

Write a short story about something on the
"All About Me" Page.

_____

_____

_____

_____

_____

_____

_____

_____

_____

_____

Brainstorming

The definition of Brainstorming is "a technique for generating ideas and solving specific problems with uncensored and nonlinear thinking, usually performed through group participation in a spontaneous discussion where all ideas are noted without assigning them value, and no proposal is selected or discarded until after the conclusion of the creative exercise." www.dictionary.com

Let your brain roam and see what great idea comes out.

Take your time. Think of many things. Get them down on paper. Brainstorm the subject to its fullest. Then review, analyze, decide and create.

Let's go!

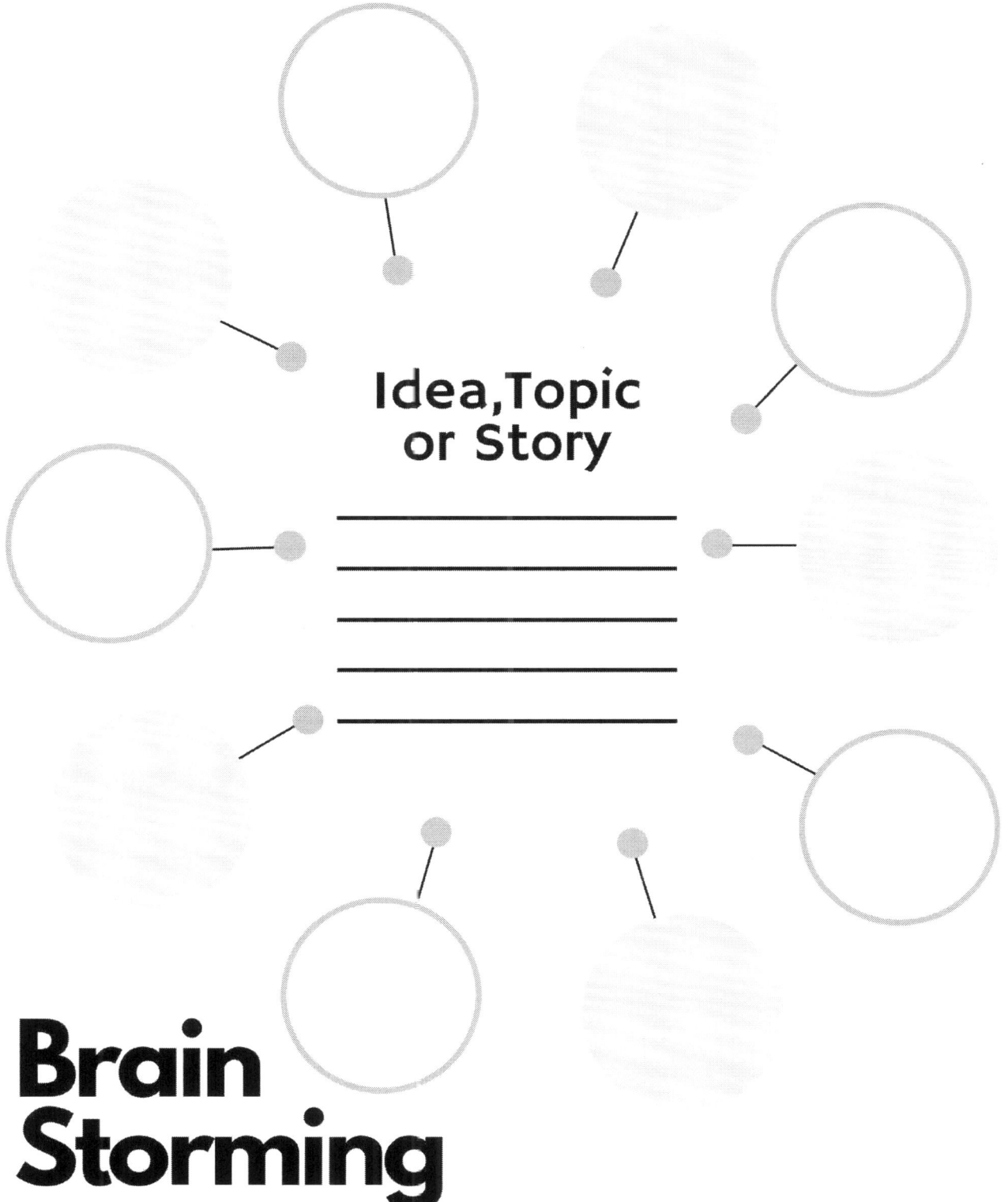

Idea, Topic
or Story

_____
_____
_____
_____
_____

Brain
Storming

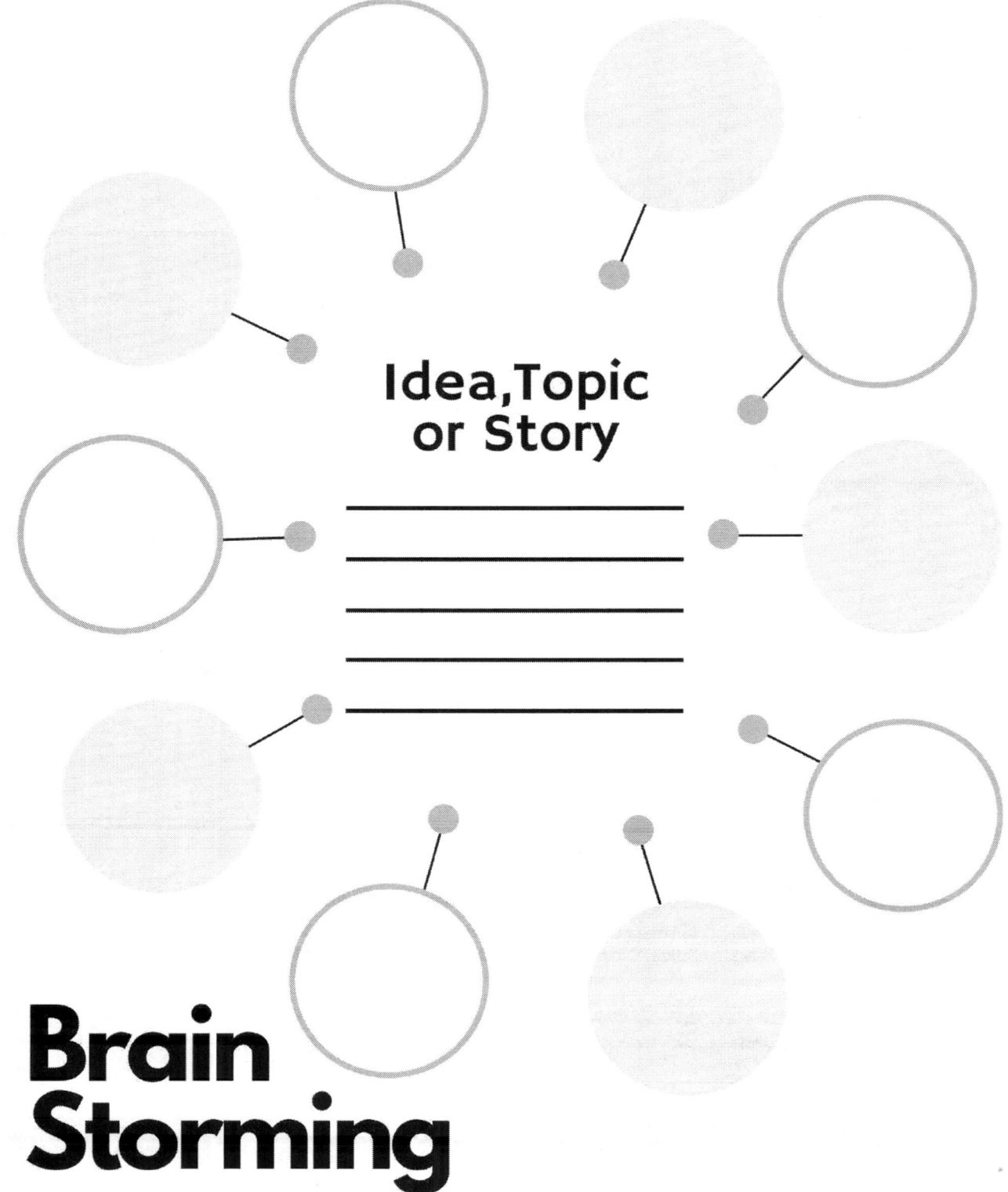

Idea, Topic
or Story

Brain
Storming

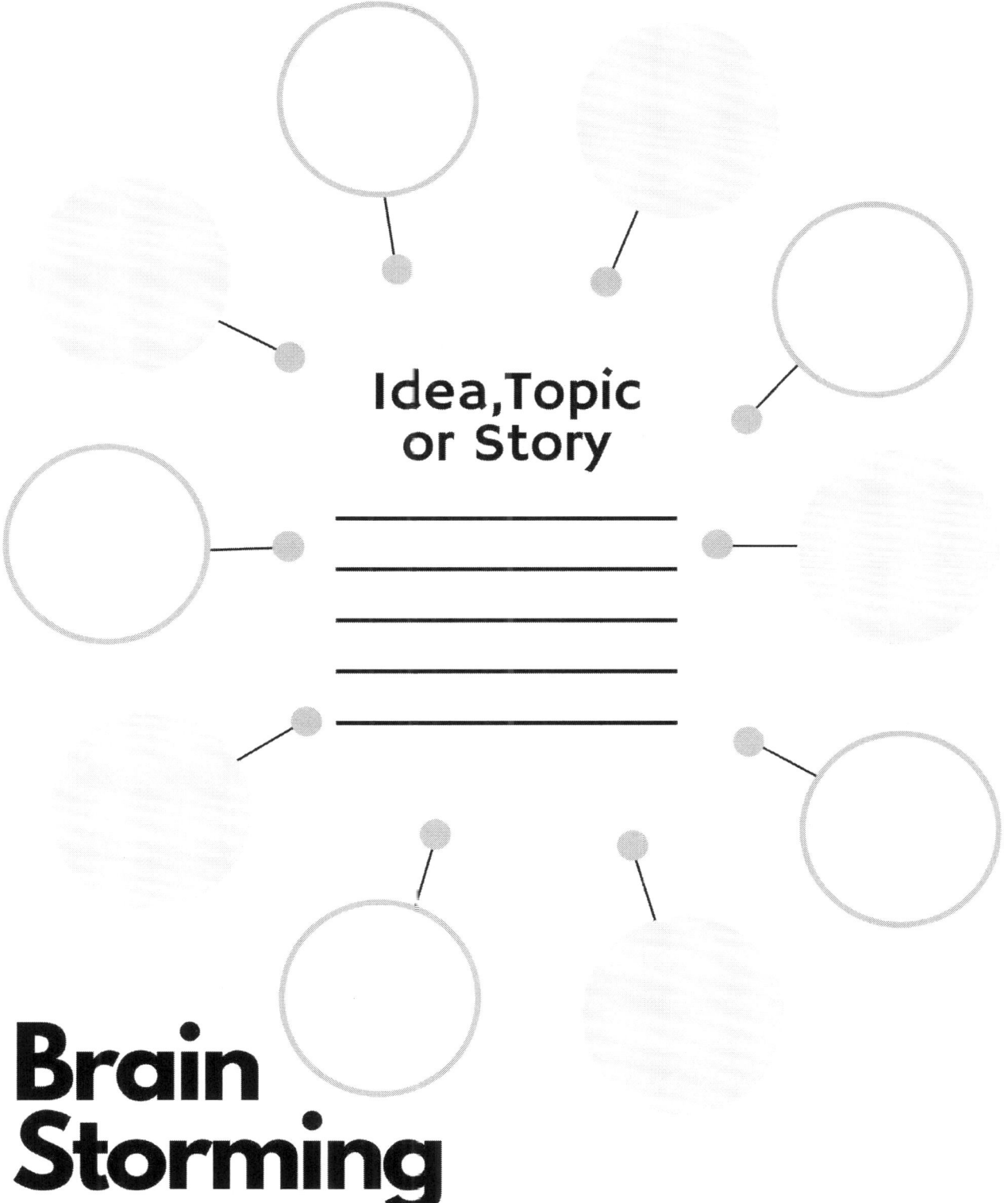

Idea,Topic
or Story

_____
_____
_____
_____
_____

**Brain
Storming**

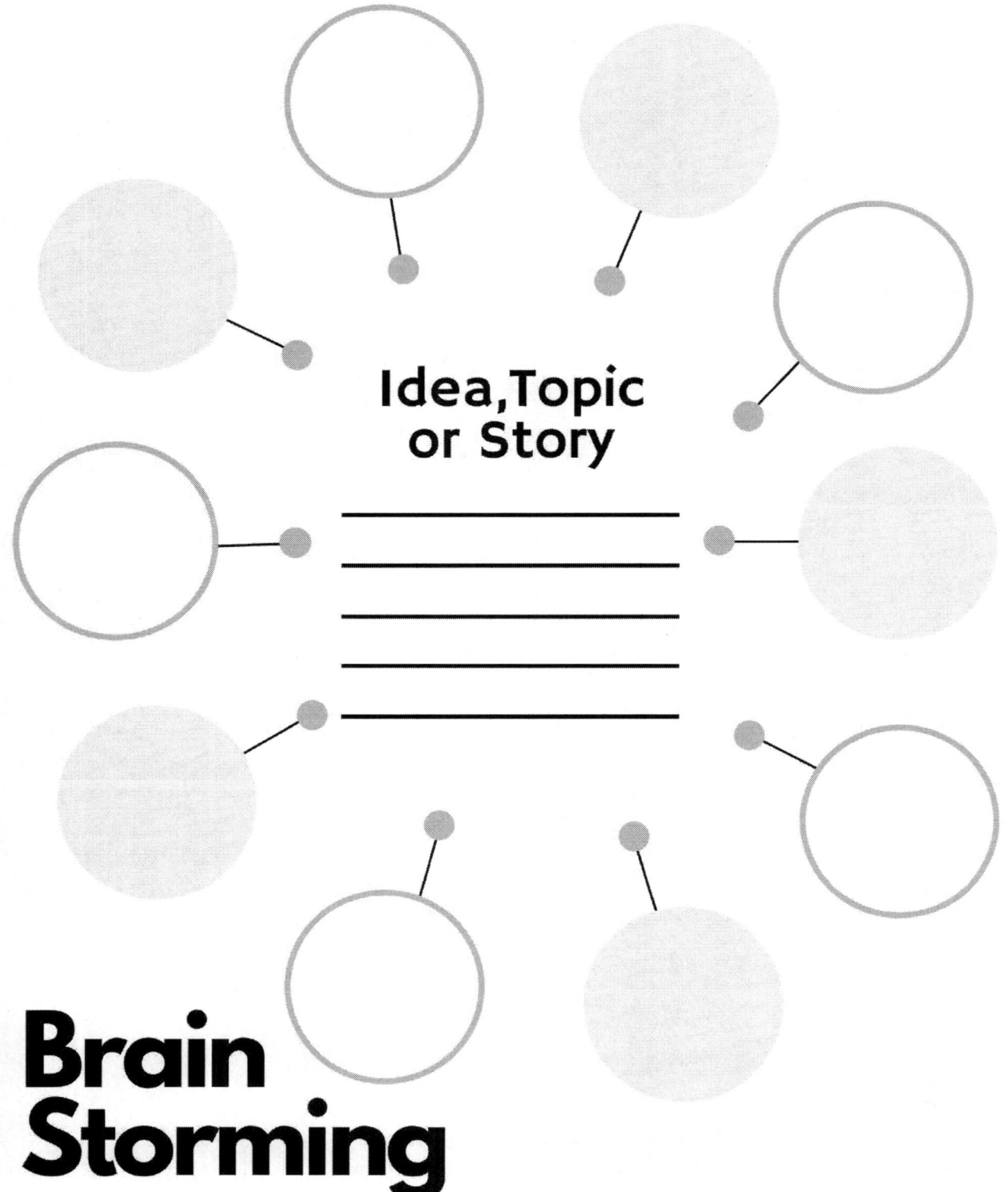

Idea, Topic
or Story

_____
_____
_____
_____
_____

Brain
Storming

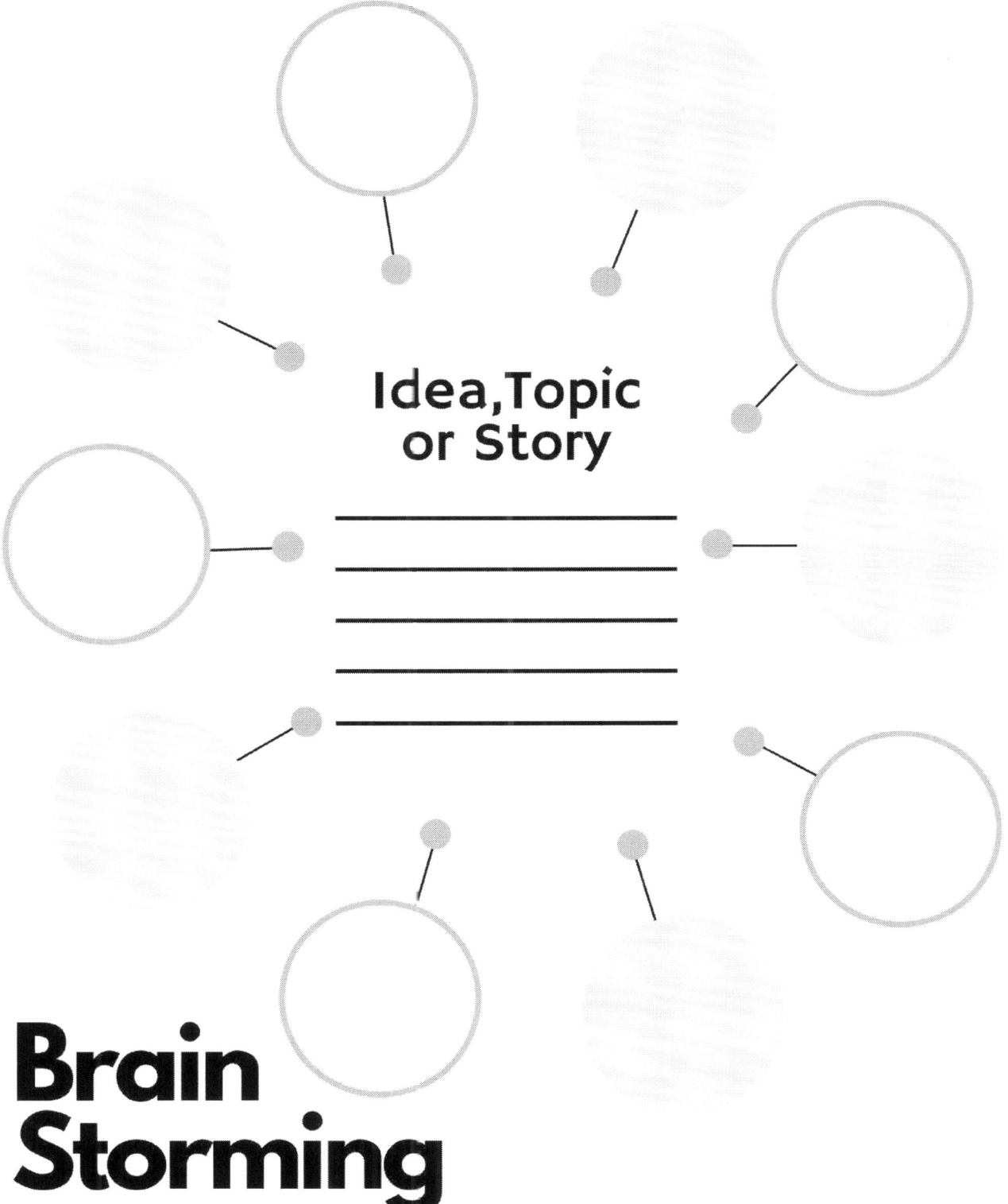

Idea, Topic or Story

_____

_____

_____

_____

_____

Brain Storming

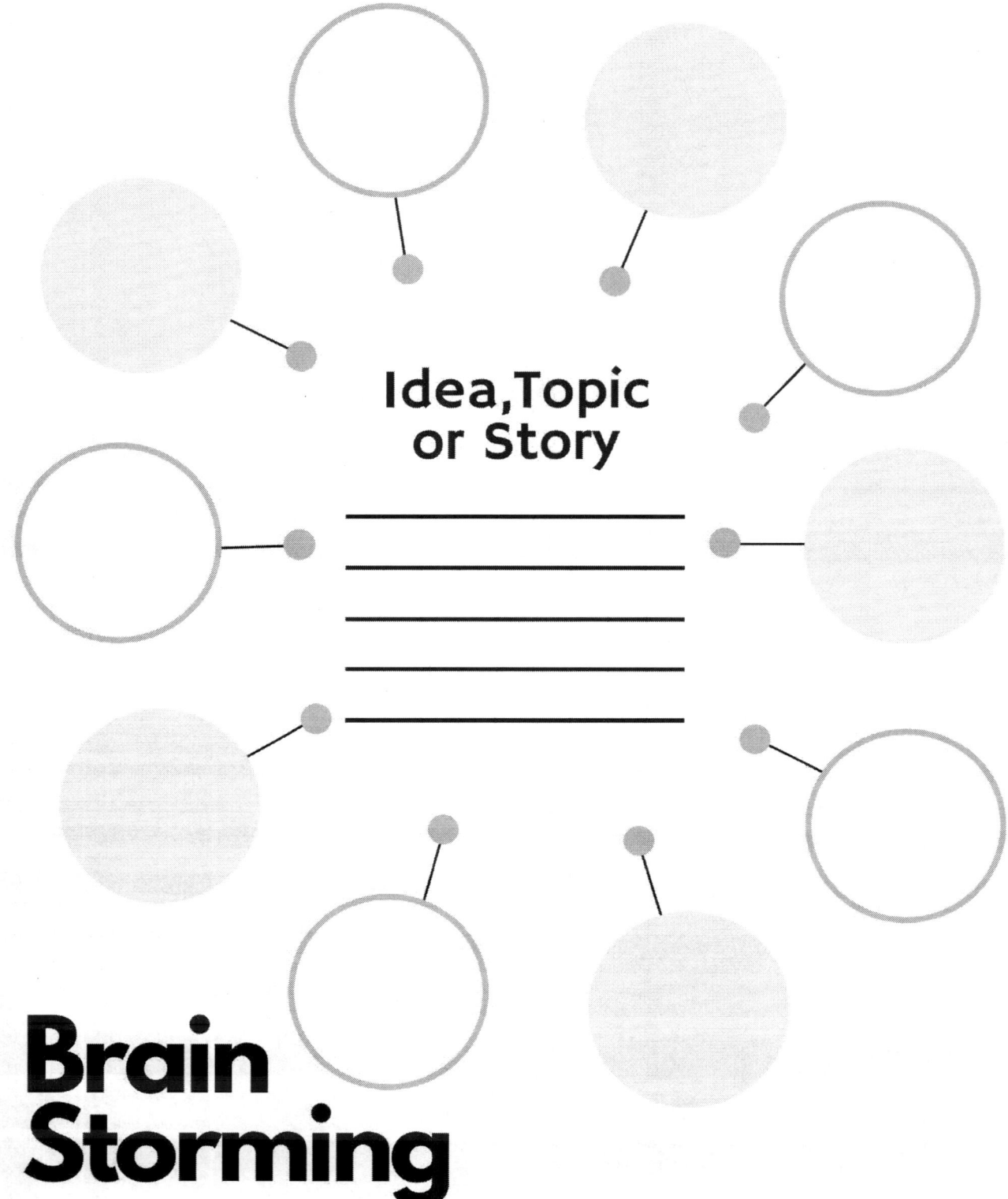

Idea, Topic or Story

Brain Storming

Let's Write a Story

When writing a great story, there are specific ingredients that should be included just like any good recipe for a great dish.

Below is a glossary of what the terms or ingredients mean for that great story. Refer to the glossary often. If you need more help, don't hesitate to email us at bkroystonpublishing@gmail.com. Let's go!

Plot

The main events of a play, novel, movie, or similar work, devised and presented by the writer as an interrelated sequence. (www.dictionary.com)

Setting

Setting is defined as the place or type of surroundings where something is positioned or where an event takes place. (www.dictionary.com)

What is or where is the setting of your fiction book? For my romance fiction book, Roberts Junction, I created a fictitious place. It is deemed to be located in Southern Indiana in the United States but there is no such place as Roberts Junction, Indiana. But what are some very familiar places or landmarks in small towns in the Mid-west of the U. S.? Walmart, grocery stores, gas station, hardware stores, etcetera. The beauty of fiction is that you can create whatever you want to exist in that town. You need to determine and/or decide on the setting because even though your scenes may be the same, where these scenes take place will be determined by the setting.

Characters

A person(s) in a novel, play, or movie. (www.dictionary.com) – Who are the people in your fiction book? Although people may change over the course of a book due to circumstances, death, life, marriage or other changes, at the beginning or onset of writing a fiction book you should have a general idea of your characters.

Some questions to ask:

Who are the main characters in this book?

What do they wear?

What do they eat?

Where do they live?

What is their career?

Major Characters

The book is yours and you can have as many characters in the book as possible but I suggest you don't have so many characters that the reader is confused about the characters and the part they play in the book. I suggest 4-6 main characters and then some sub-characters, side kick characters or minor characters whom you may introduce mysteriously for one page and not mention them again until they have their own book.

Minor Characters

Are there any minor or side-kick characters to the main/major characters? These people can play a major role in developing the main character, revealing the plot, maintaining and unveiling the theme or may take a major role in the next addition of the series or have their own series. I also like to be mysterious and write minor characters as the best friend who could turn on the main character, trick them or betray them in the end. It's my book, I write like I want to, but in your book, the minor character may and could play many roles. You decide because you are the author. Let's go!

Outline

An outline is an important resource or tool needed to write fiction. Why? Because you need an even tighter framework and structure for the specific scenes or acts that you want to convey in fiction. The outline can help you begin the book, figure out what will happen in the middle and how the book should end. Making sure the book flows, makes sense throughout each transition and has an ending that gets us to a specific destination is critical. After the basic outline is determined, I also compile a profile of each character as well as the overall book itself.

Ending

It is amazing that the ending comes after the outline and before scene one begins. Why? Because, trust me, I wasted time developing characters, outlining the story and determining the plot but didn't know how it ended. Without an ending, you won't know how to get the characters to the end because you don't have a complete road map to the destination of the end. Is it a happy ending? Is it open-ended and you don't know what happened at the end? Is it a sad ending and catastrophe happens to all of the characters or does it end weird, leaving you thinking and wondering? No matter the end, decide on an ending before you start determining the scenes or storyboard of the story. It helps, I promise you.

Scene

The word scene is taken directly from film and the movies. Scene is defined as a "unit of action or a segment of a story in a play, motion picture, or television show." (www.dictionary.com) I suggest the organizational structure of the movies to help best come up with scenes for a fiction book. These particular group of activities or actions in a particular scene can also be transferred and transformed into chapters. So in Scene 1 or Chapter 1, what happens?

The Plot...

_____

_____

_____

_____

_____

_____

_____

_____

_____

_____

The Setting....

The Characters...

_____

_____

_____

_____

_____

_____

_____

_____

_____

Major Character...

_____

_____

_____

_____

_____

_____

_____

_____

_____

_____

_____

Minor Character...

_____

_____

_____

_____

_____

_____

_____

_____

_____

_____

_____

Outline...

Outline...

_____

_____

_____

_____

_____

_____

_____

_____

_____

_____

Ending...

_____

_____

_____

_____

_____

_____

_____

_____

_____

_____

_____

Scene 1...

_____

_____

_____

_____

_____

_____

_____

_____

_____

_____

Scene 2...

Scene 3...

_____

_____

_____

_____

_____

_____

_____

_____

_____

_____

_____

_____

Scene 4...

Scene 5...

_____

_____

_____

_____

_____

_____

_____

_____

_____

_____

_____

Scene 6...

_____

_____

_____

_____

_____

_____

_____

_____

_____

Scene 7...

_____

_____

_____

_____

_____

_____

_____

_____

_____

_____

Scene 8...

Scene 9...

_____

_____

_____

_____

_____

_____

_____

_____

_____

_____

_____

Scene 10...

More Scenes...

_____

_____

_____

_____

_____

_____

_____

_____

_____

_____

More Scenes...

More Scenes...

More Scenes...

More Scenes...

_____

_____

_____

_____

_____

_____

_____

_____

_____

_____

_____

Let's Draw

Music Composition And Lyrics

As someone who writes music, I can't tell you what comes first, the music or the lyrics. Why? Because I get both in my head at the exact same time.

Just in case you read music, I have provided the staff. If you are like me, you can write down the lyrics/words but the music you may have to record on your phone and then have a musician whom you trust to create the music for you. Special thanks to every musician who has ever taken what was inside of my head and made it beautiful.

Open your heart. Open your head. Open these pages and write down what you hear. Let's go!

Lyrics

Lyrics

Lyrics

Lyrics

Lyrics

Dance and Movement

This is an area of creativity that I literally know nothing about but applaud a dancer loudly when I see it done well. I honestly had to look it up (Google Search) to see what was necessary to be able to plan out choreography. "A standard 32 beat phrase of music, which is made of four 8-counts, will have four rectangles on each line. To find out what a standard chorus would look like, visit this website:" https://dance.mandigould.com/choreography/

I am mesmerized by dance. I watch it and wonder how the choreographer decides which way for the dancers to move their bodies and where to position them on stage. Now it's your turn. Let's go!

Planning
And
Goal Setting

A goal without a plan is just a wish. – Antoine de Saint-Exupéry

WHAT ARE YOUR FIVE MAJOR GOALS FOR THIS YEAR?

Goal 1:

Goal 2:

Goal 3:

Goal 4:

Goal 5:

Month:

Sunday	Monday	Tuesday	Wednesday	Thursday	Friday	Saturday

Notes

Goals Planner

JANUARY

FEBRUARY

MARCH

APRIL

MAY

JUNE

JULY

AUGUST

SEPTEMBER

OCTOBER

NOVEMBER

DECEMBER

Goal:

Start: End:

ACTION STEPS

MILESTONES

SUMMARY

Month:

Sunday	Monday	Tuesday	Wednesday	Thursday	Friday	Saturday

Notes

Goals Planner

JANUARY	FEBRUARY

MARCH	APRIL

MAY	JUNE

JULY	AUGUST

SEPTEMBER	OCTOBER

NOVEMBER	DECEMBER

Goal:

Start: End:

ACTION STEPS

MILESTONES

SUMMARY

Month:

Sunday	Monday	Tuesday	Wednesday	Thursday	Friday	Saturday

Notes

Goals Planner

JANUARY

FEBRUARY

MARCH

APRIL

MAY

JUNE

JULY

AUGUST

SEPTEMBER

OCTOBER

NOVEMBER

DECEMBER

Goal:

Start: End:

ACTION STEPS

MILESTONES

SUMMARY

Month:

Sunday	Monday	Tuesday	Wednesday	Thursday	Friday	Saturday

Notes

Goals Planner

JANUARY

FEBRUARY

MARCH

APRIL

MAY

JUNE

JULY

AUGUST

SEPTEMBER

OCTOBER

NOVEMBER

DECEMBER

Goal:

Start: End:

ACTION STEPS

MILESTONES

SUMMARY

- ○
- ○
- ○
- ○
- ○
- ○
- ○

Month:

Sunday	Monday	Tuesday	Wednesday	Thursday	Friday	Saturday

Notes

Goals Planner

JANUARY
_____
_____
_____
_____

FEBRUARY
_____
_____
_____
_____

MARCH
_____
_____
_____
_____

APRIL
_____
_____
_____
_____

MAY
_____
_____
_____
_____

JUNE
_____
_____
_____
_____

JULY
_____
_____
_____
_____

AUGUST
_____
_____
_____
_____

SEPTEMBER
_____
_____
_____
_____

OCTOBER
_____
_____
_____
_____

NOVEMBER
_____
_____
_____
_____

DECEMBER
_____
_____
_____
_____

Goal: _____

Start: _____   End: _____

ACTION STEPS
_____
_____
_____
_____

MILESTONES

SUMMARY
- _____
- _____
- _____
- _____
- _____
- _____
- _____

Month:

Sunday	Monday	Tuesday	Wednesday	Thursday	Friday	Saturday

Notes

Goals Planner

JANUARY

FEBRUARY

MARCH

APRIL

MAY

JUNE

JULY

AUGUST

SEPTEMBER

OCTOBER

NOVEMBER

DECEMBER

Goal:

Start: End:

ACTION STEPS

MILESTONES

SUMMARY

Month:

Sunday	Monday	Tuesday	Wednesday	Thursday	Friday	Saturday

Notes

Goals Planner

JANUARY
_____
_____
_____
_____

FEBRUARY
_____
_____
_____
_____

MARCH
_____
_____
_____
_____

APRIL
_____
_____
_____
_____

MAY
_____
_____
_____
_____

JUNE
_____
_____
_____
_____

JULY
_____
_____
_____
_____

AUGUST
_____
_____
_____
_____

SEPTEMBER
_____
_____
_____
_____

OCTOBER
_____
_____
_____
_____

NOVEMBER
_____
_____
_____
_____

DECEMBER
_____
_____
_____
_____

Goal: _____

Start: _____   End: _____

ACTION STEPS

_____
_____
_____
_____
_____
_____

MILESTONES

SUMMARY

○ _____
○ _____
○ _____
○ _____
○ _____
○ _____
○ _____

Month:

Sunday	Monday	Tuesday	Wednesday	Thursday	Friday	Saturday

Notes

Goals Planner

JANUARY

_____
_____
_____
_____

FEBRUARY

_____
_____
_____
_____

MARCH

_____
_____
_____
_____

APRIL

_____
_____
_____
_____

MAY

_____
_____
_____
_____

JUNE

_____
_____
_____
_____

JULY

_____
_____
_____
_____

AUGUST

_____
_____
_____
_____

SEPTEMBER

_____
_____
_____
_____

OCTOBER

_____
_____
_____
_____

NOVEMBER

_____
_____
_____
_____

DECEMBER

_____
_____
_____
_____

Goal: _____

Start: _____   End: _____

ACTION STEPS

_____
_____
_____
_____

MILESTONES

_____
_____
_____
_____
_____

SUMMARY

○ _____
○ _____
○ _____
○ _____
○ _____
○ _____
○ _____

Month:

Sunday	Monday	Tuesday	Wednesday	Thursday	Friday	Saturday

Notes

Goals Planner

JANUARY

_____
_____
_____
_____

FEBRUARY

_____
_____
_____
_____

MARCH

_____
_____
_____
_____

APRIL

_____
_____
_____
_____

MAY

_____
_____
_____
_____

JUNE

_____
_____
_____
_____

JULY

_____
_____
_____
_____

AUGUST

_____
_____
_____
_____

SEPTEMBER

_____
_____
_____
_____

OCTOBER

_____
_____
_____
_____

NOVEMBER

_____
_____
_____
_____

DECEMBER

_____
_____
_____
_____

Goal: _____

Start: _____ End: _____

ACTION STEPS

_____
_____
_____
_____
_____

MILESTONES

SUMMARY

○ _____
○ _____
○ _____
○ _____
○ _____
○ _____
○ _____

Month:

Sunday	Monday	Tuesday	Wednesday	Thursday	Friday	Saturday

Notes

Goals Planner

JANUARY
_____
_____
_____
_____

FEBRUARY
_____
_____
_____
_____

MARCH
_____
_____
_____
_____

APRIL
_____
_____
_____
_____

MAY
_____
_____
_____
_____

JUNE
_____
_____
_____
_____

JULY
_____
_____
_____
_____

AUGUST
_____
_____
_____
_____

SEPTEMBER
_____
_____
_____
_____

OCTOBER
_____
_____
_____
_____

NOVEMBER
_____
_____
_____
_____

DECEMBER
_____
_____
_____
_____

Goal: _____

Start: _____ End: _____

ACTION STEPS

_____
_____
_____
_____
_____

MILESTONES

SUMMARY

○ _____
○ _____
○ _____
○ _____
○ _____
○ _____
○ _____

Month:

Sunday	Monday	Tuesday	Wednesday	Thursday	Friday	Saturday

Notes

Goals Planner

JANUARY

_____
_____
_____
_____

FEBRUARY

_____
_____
_____
_____

MARCH

_____
_____
_____
_____

APRIL

_____
_____
_____
_____

MAY

_____
_____
_____
_____

JUNE

_____
_____
_____
_____

JULY

_____
_____
_____
_____

AUGUST

_____
_____
_____
_____

SEPTEMBER

_____
_____
_____
_____

OCTOBER

_____
_____
_____
_____

NOVEMBER

_____
_____
_____
_____

DECEMBER

_____
_____
_____
_____

Goal: _____

Start: _____   End: _____

ACTION STEPS

_____
_____
_____
_____
_____

MILESTONES

SUMMARY

○ _____
○ _____
○ _____
○ _____
○ _____
○ _____
○ _____

Month:

Sunday	Monday	Tuesday	Wednesday	Thursday	Friday	Saturday

Notes

Goals Planner

JANUARY

_____
_____
_____

FEBRUARY

_____
_____
_____

MARCH

_____
_____
_____
_____

APRIL

_____
_____
_____
_____

MAY

_____
_____
_____
_____

JUNE

_____
_____
_____
_____

JULY

_____
_____
_____
_____

AUGUST

_____
_____
_____
_____

SEPTEMBER

_____
_____
_____
_____

OCTOBER

_____
_____
_____
_____

NOVEMBER

_____
_____
_____
_____

DECEMBER

_____
_____
_____
_____

Goal: _____

Start: _____   End: _____

ACTION STEPS

_____
_____
_____
_____

MILESTONES

SUMMARY

○ _____
○ _____
○ _____
○ _____
○ _____
○ _____
○ _____

Journaling and Notes

_____

_____

_____

_____

_____

_____

_____

_____

_____

_____

_____

_____

_____

_____

_____

_____

_____

_____

_____

_____

_____

_____

_____

_____

_____

_____

_____

_____

_____

_____

_____

_____

_____

_____

_____

_____

_____

_____

_____

_____

_____

_____

_____

_____

_____

_____

_____

_____

_____

_____

_____

_____

_____

_____

_____

_____

_____

_____

_____

_____

_____

_____

_____

_____

_____

_____

_____

_____

_____

_____

_____

_____

_____

_____

_____

_____

_____

_____

_____

_____

_____

_____

_____

_____

_____

_____

_____

_____

_____

_____

_____

_____

_____

_____

_____

_____

_____

_____

_____

_____

_____

_____

_____

_____

_____

_____

_____

NOTES

NOTES

NOTES

NOTES

NOTES

NOTES

NOTES

NOTES

NOTES

NOTES

Other Books by

Julia A. Royston

Purchase at
www.juliaroystonstore.com

Made in the USA
Columbia, SC
28 September 2024

43044662R00072